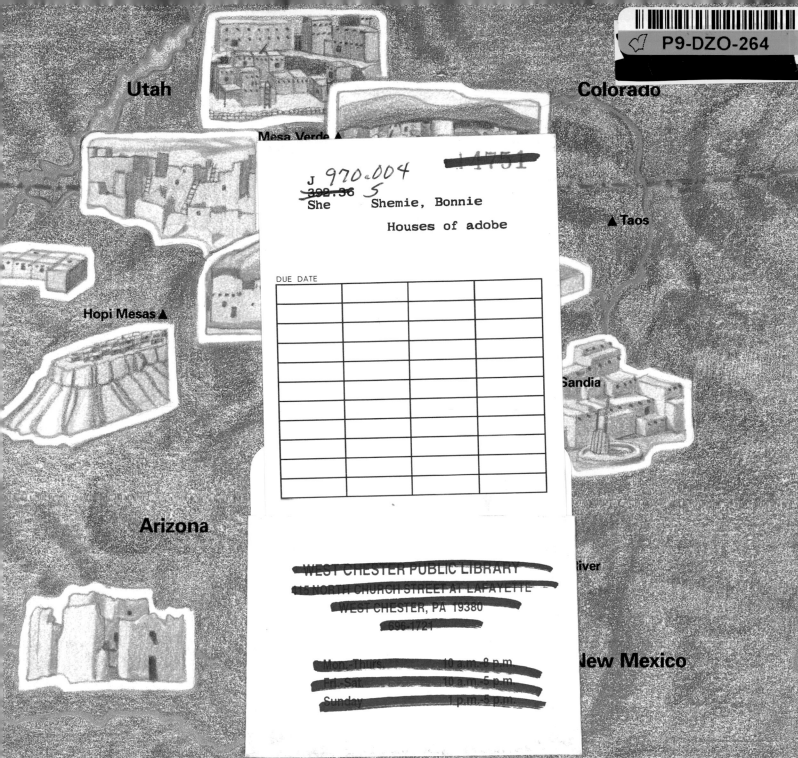

Utah
Colorado
Mesa Verde ▲
▲ Taos
Hopi Mesas ▲
Sandia
Arizona
New Mexico

Native dwellings: the Southwest

Bonnie Shemie

Houses of adobe

Tundra Books

Also by Bonnie Shemie:

Houses of snow, skin and bones: Native dwellings of the Far North
Houses of bark: Native dwellings of the Woodland Indians
Houses of hide and earth: Native Dwellings of the Plains Indians
Houses of wood: Native Dwellings of the Northwest Coast
Mounds of earth and shell: Native sites of the Southeast

Published in Canada by Tundra Books, Montreal, Quebec H3Z 2N2

Published in the United States by Tundra Books of Northern New York, Plattsburgh, N.Y. 12901

Distributed in the United Kingdom by Ragged Bears Ltd., Andover, Hampshire SP11 9HX

Library of Congress Catalog Number: 93-61789

Canadian Cataloging in Publication Data:

Shemie, Bonnie, 1949-
    Houses of adobe

ISBN 0-88776-330-8 hardcover 5 4 3 2 1
ISBN 0-88776-353-7 paperback 5 4 3 2 1

(Issued also in French under the title: *Maisons d'adobe*. ISBN 0-88776-331-6)

    1. Indians of North America- Southwest, New- Dwellings-Juvenile literature. 2. Stone houses-Southwest, New-Juvenile literature. 3. Adobe houses-Southwest, New-Juvenile literature. I. Title.

E78.S7S43 1994   j392'.36'008997079   C94-900047-7

Printed in Hong Kong by South China Printing Co. Ltd.

Acknowledgments:
The author/illustrator would like to thank Dr. Karen Dohm, Museum Specialist, Anthropology, at the Smithsonian Institution, Washington, D.C., and Dr. Katherine A. Spielmann, Associate Professor, Department of Anthropology, Arizona State University, Tempe, Arizona, for their comments, suggestions and advice. She also wishes to acknowledge the help of the people at Chaco Culture National Historic Park, New Mexico; the Maxwell Museum of Anthropology, Albuquerque, New Mexico; Mesa Verde National Park, Colorado; Taos Pueblo, Taos, New Mexico; and to thank the libraries of McGill University, Montreal, for their cooperation.

Bibliography:
Ferguson, William and Rohn, Arthur H., *Anasazi Ruins of the Southwest in Color*, Albuquerque: University of New Mexico Press, 1987.
Houk, Rose, *Anasazi, Hohokam, Mogollon, Salado, Sinagua*, Tucson: Southwest Parks and Monuments Association, 1992.
Nabokov, Peter and Easton, Robert, *Native American Architecture*, New York: Oxford University Press, 1989.
Scully, Vincent, *Pueblo: Mountain, Village, Dance*, New York: Viking Press, 1975.
Sturtevant, William, ed., *Handbook of North American Indians*, vols. 9-10 (Southwest), Washington, D.C.: Smithsonian Institution Press, 1978.

The Southwest

Long before the morning sun was high enough to brighten the canyon floor, the two families were gone. They left only a few scattered remains of their cooking fire and a trail of footprints in the dried riverbed. Carrying skins, weapons and a little food, they lived by gathering plants and hunting. If they were near canyons, they took refuge under overhanging cliffs. If they were out in the open plain, they built small huts or set up tents.

These were the first people to roam the mountains and plateaus of the southwest United States. Through the following centuries their descendants built the longest enduring — and some of the most fascinating — Native architecture in North America.

They built homes into the sides of steep canyon walls and cities surrounded by vast road systems. They molded clay into adobe bricks, and built dwellings that housed many families, like today's apartment buildings.

The heartland of this culture is in the Four Corners region, where Arizona, New Mexico, Colorado and Utah join. Dusty plains, scarred with dried riverbeds, roar to life when a flash flood occurs. The plains abruptly give way to snow-capped mountains or rise into tabletop land cut through with deep canyons. In this harsh and beautiful land these people used the materials around them to create shelters that awe us with their ingenuity.

The southwestern states gave rise to America's oldest enduring architecture.

In AD 1300, a Hopi village overlooked the dry, rugged landscape of Arizona.

The first Americans

Twelve thousand years ago, the Four Corners region looked a little like an African savanna of today. The first Americans may have hunted mammoth, bison and antelope that grazed among the many lakes and rivers, as well as small game such as rabbit. Gradually the land became drier, and the big land animals moved on or became extinct. People adapted. They concentrated on smaller game and the vegetation around them: nourishing kernels, healing herbs and edible berries. They stored these foods in stone-lined pits in the floors of caves so they would be less dependent on the changing seasons and the availability of animals.

Three thousand years ago, wanderers and traders came north from the civilizations in Mexico. They brought dried corn with them and the people of the Southwest started to grow, harvest and preserve it. To cultivate corn, a family had to stay in one place for at least part of the year. People started to build permanent dwellings that could serve them for years, not a few nights or weeks.

The pit house

These first dwellings are called pit houses by archaeologists because the floor was dug a few feet into the ground to form a round or oblong pit. A strong wood frame was raised in the center to support a roof made of timbers. This was covered, first with brush and then a thick blanket of earth. Entry was either through a small passage on the side, or down a ladder that extended through the smoke hole on top. A pit house was a snug but smoky place in winter.

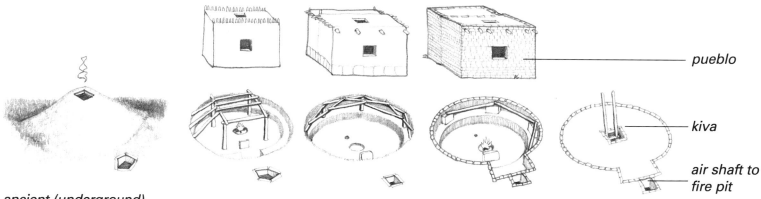

ancient (underground) pit house

pueblo

kiva

air shaft to fire pit

Evolution of the kiva and above-ground dwellings (pueblo)

Moving above ground

A settlement in AD 700 is surrounded by fields of squash and beans and corn. The boys are guarding the fields from hungry crows while gathering firewood. The men are out hunting. In the shade of the pit house, a child is kneading soft chunks of clay that she and her mother have collected for making pottery. A stew simmers on an open fire. The mother is shelling pinyon nuts and acorns and putting them in a basket woven from the fibers of the yucca plant. The grandmother is laying out juniper berries in the sun to dry. She keeps the dried food in a small stone and wood storage room built above ground and plastered over with clay mud.

Soon it was realized that the storage rooms could be lived in. People began building them in rows, sometimes adding rooms to the back. Later they would be stacked box-like on top of each other.

But the pit houses were not abandoned. Each row of dwellings had one or two deep pit rooms in front. These were used as meeting places and ceremonial chambers by members of a related group, or clan. On cold winter nights, the inhabitants probably all slept here, wrapped in rabbit fur or feather blankets. These special rooms are known as *kivas* and are still used as meeting places today.

When the Spanish later saw these settlements, they called them *pueblos*, or villages, because of their resemblance to the houses and courtyards in Spain.

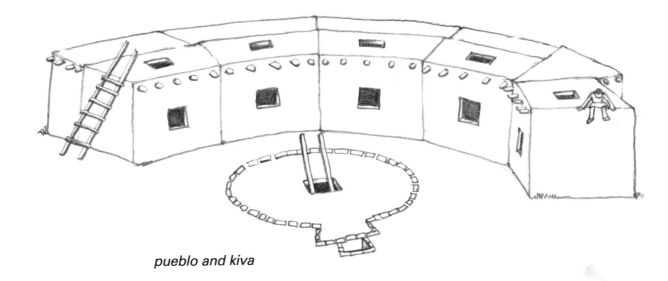

pueblo and kiva

In Chaco Canyon, a "great house" of 800 rooms could shelter 1,000 people.

A 400-mile road system linked these large structures with distant villages.

The great houses of Chaco Canyon

By AD 800, the people of the Southwest had refined their hunting tools, domesticated turkeys and made pottery that heated quickly. They also added cotton to their vast fields of corn, squash and beans. With these advances, the population grew and a building boom was on.

One of the results was an architecture that can still be seen today in a remote part of New Mexico called Chaco Canyon. Around AD 900, people started building enormous stone structures we call "great houses."

The biggest, Pueblo Bonito, had 800 rooms and 32 kivas, and could house a thousand people. Skillful masons built walls that were four feet thick at the base and rose as high as four stories.

These were planned communities that took years to build. Four hundred miles of road connected the canyon's great houses to distant villages. The system remains an impressive achievement. Roads are straight, sometimes cut five feet deep into earth or bedrock. Some have masonry borders, others have steps cut into solid rock that lead up out of the valley.

These roads seem to have linked many places. Items have been found that suggest that Chaco Canyon was the center of a large trading network — painted pottery from other regions, shell ornaments from the Pacific coast, copper bells from Mexico and the remains of tropical birds.

cooking vessel
(pockmarked to increase heating surface)

Chaco Canyon pottery   *ceremonial bowl*

Charting the sun and seasons

Only recently did we discover that the people of Chaco Canyon possessed another kind of knowledge. It was hidden for a thousand years in two petroglyphs carved into the rock high on Fajada Butte at the end of the canyon. A petroglyph is a design made by pecking away the surface of a boulder with a hard, hand-held rock. In 1977, an artist examining the petroglyphs discovered that two spirals, a small one and a big one, mark the sun's yearly cycle.

It was the first day of summer and just about noon. As the artist looked, a shaft of light pierced the center of the larger spiral for a period of about 18 minutes. On this day and at this time, the sun is at its highest point in the sky. Someone a thousand years ago knew how to recognize the longest and shortest days of the year. He or she had ingeniously carved the spirals behind the giant fallen sandstone slabs to mark the summer and winter solstices and even the spring and fall equinoxes (the two days of the year when day and night are both twelve hours long).

Sunlight hits the spirals on an ancient calendar found on Fajada Butte, Chaco Canyon, during the autumnal equinox, one of only two days a year when day and night are both twelve hours long.

In the 1100's people began to move out of Chaco Canyon, and by the early 1200's, it was entirely abandoned. The population had increased. Over-farming and drought had depleted the soil. People had to find new places to live.

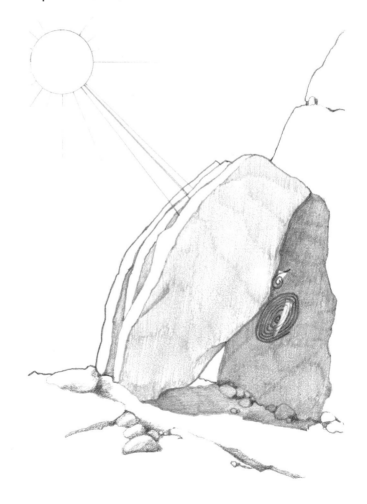

11

Narrow paths cut into the steep canyon walls of Colorado by the cliff dwellers

made climbing difficult and dangerous but offered protection against enemy attacks.

The cliff dwellings of Mesa Verde

Even more astonishing than the great houses of New Mexico are the cliff dwellings. One can stand on top of a mesa in Colorado, look across a canyon hundreds of feet deep, and see houses built right into the cliff wall on the opposite side.

Why did people choose to build in such a dangerous place? Or live where all provisions had to be carried by hand over treacherous paths? Because the site, though dangerous and difficult for them, was even more so for their enemies. The narrow paths, some only footholds carved into the rock, could be easily defended or cut off in case of attack. Another advantage was the cliff overhang which protected them from the weather.

One of the best preserved cliff dwellings is Spruce Tree House. It has 114 rooms and eight kivas. The kivas are round and built entirely underground; their roofs function as a courtyard. They are surrounded on one, two or three sides by living quarters. Some of the small doorways were built wider at the top than at the bottom, so a person carrying a bundle on his back could pass through. Second story rooms sometimes had balconies and were reached by a ladder. Crops were planted on the ground on top of the cliff. Unlike Chaco Canyon, the towns of Mesa Verde were not planned out ahead, and rooms were added and changed haphazardly.

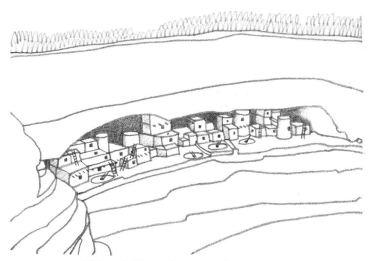

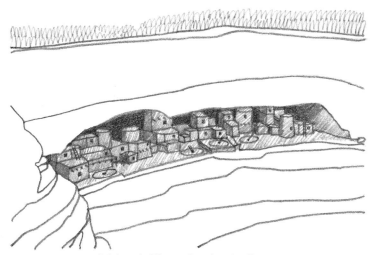

14   *winter — midday (village is sunny)*

summer — midday (village is shaded)

Storing water in a dry land

The cliff dwellers devised many artful ways of preserving water. It didn't rain very often, but when it did, the water came in torrents, causing flash floods. Low dams were built on the mesa tops to trap and divert the floodwater. Water seeped down through the porous sandstone until it hit solid shale and could sink no further. It then searched across the top of the shale until it found an opening in the side of the canyon wall and came out as a spring. Those who had such a spring in their settlements were lucky. Other people had to walk long distances over steep paths.

The Mesa Verde dwellings were occupied for about five generations and were abandoned by AD 1300. A drought had lasted twenty-five years. The soil was exhausted. The area was picked clean of vegetation because trees were cut to provide fuel. People were forced to move away.

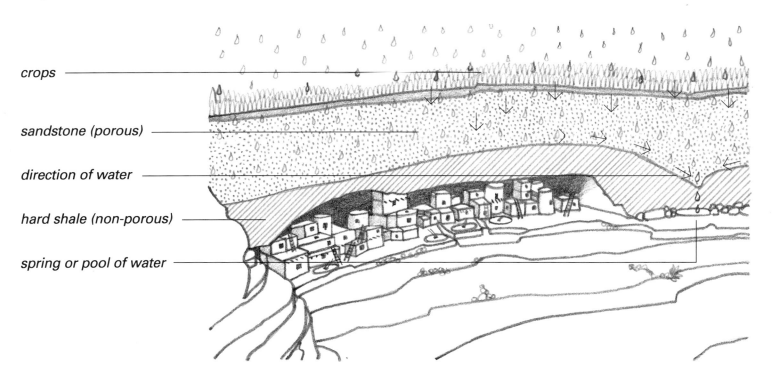

crops

sandstone (porous)

direction of water

hard shale (non-porous)

spring or pool of water

The women layered stones and adobe bricks, then plastered the walls smooth.

Everyone helped in the building of a pueblo. The men brought logs for the roof.

The pueblo

The settlements of Chaco Canyon and the cliff dwellings of Mesa Verde were forgotten for centuries after they were deserted. Trees grew up in the canyons and hid the cliff dwellings. Roof beams rotted, stone walls crumbled, canyon walls collapsed. By the time the first Spanish explorers passed through in 1540, most of the Indians had regrouped into pueblos around the Rio Grande in north central New Mexico, at Zuni and Acoma, and on the Hopi mesas. These towns consisted of large apartment houses, one to five stories high, built around plazas.

In a Hopi pueblo the rooms used for living, sleeping and food preparation usually opened onto the outside. Inner, harder to reach rooms were for storage. Openings in the walls and floors connected the rooms of a family. A room was added, a storage room altered, as the need arose. Each clan, made up of a group of related families, maintained a kiva within, or close to, the pueblo.

Building a house of adobe

We know that by 150 years ago, when more accounts were written about the pueblo dwellings, women owned the houses. When a woman married, her husband moved in with her family. When the couple needed a dwelling of their own, they chose a place near the wife's mother or sister. Then the man and his male relatives and friends went far away to the forest to cut timber for the roof.

The women made bricks for the walls. First they built a fire of sagebrush and sedge grass, two plants that grow abundantly in the Southwest. When the fire was almost burned out, they threw water on it and mixed the ashes with sandy clay to form bricks. These harden in the sun into the tough building material called adobe.

The building began with a ritual. A village elder placed sacred feathers under each cornerstone of the new house and said a blessing for the safety of the inhabitants. He then sprinkled cornmeal where the walls would be built, while chanting a traditional song.

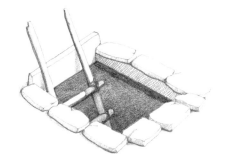

downspout

roof opening

roof opening covered w. stone slab during rain or sno

Women did much of the construction and all of the plastering. Men helped in the heavy work. Layers of stone or adobe bricks were laid for the walls, using as little mud mortar as possible. Small stones were carefully pounded into place between the large stones to make the walls as smooth as possible.

Men positioned the big roof timbers on top of the walls. These were overlaid with smaller poles covered with brush and then mud. A low wall or parapet was then constructed along the edge of the roof to direct rainwater. Downspouts made from an old grinding stone, broken pottery or a concave piece of wood allowed water to escape during a downpour.

Adobe could crack and wash away in the violent rain storms of the Southwest. It required continuous maintenance and repair. Even inside walls had to be replastered every few years. The women used a white paint made of gypsum ground to a powder and mixed with water. An unpainted band was left around the bottom of the wall, like a baseboard, where the wall could not be kept clean because of floor dirt.

Some of the ancient pueblos are still lived in today. The Hopi pueblo at Old Oraibi, Arizona, has been occupied since AD 1150. It is the oldest continuously inhabited town in the United States.

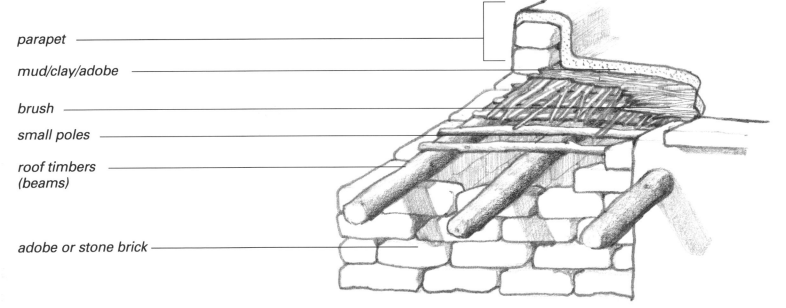

parapet

mud/clay/adobe

brush

small poles

roof timbers
(beams)

adobe or stone brick

The pueblo was America's first apartment building, housing whole communities.

As families grew larger, rooms were added as needed for shelter and storage.

Inside the pueblo

If you were visiting one of these pueblos 200 years ago, you would enter by climbing a ladder to a second story terrace. No doors are on the first floor, to protect the pueblo from intruders. In case of attack, the ladder is pulled up. From the sunny terrace you enter a room lit only by the light coming through the small doorway. Pueblos have few openings to the outside to keep the temperature even, neither too hot in the summer nor too cold in the winter. Window openings were covered in winter with slabs of selenite, a form of transparent gypsum, that let in the sun. When it got very cold, openings were sealed up altogether.

In a corner fireplace rests a blackened cooking pot. Above it a hood and chimney take away the smoke. Fires are small by necessity. The chimney flue is made of poles covered with clay and must not be overheated. Also, wood is scarce and must be conserved.

The room is simple and orderly. Along two walls a raised portion of the floor serves as shelves. Blankets that had been spread on the floor for sleeping now lie folded on one. The other is devoted to kitchen utensils: gourd dippers, grass brooms, a mortar and pestle for grinding seeds and nuts. A niche in the wall holds clean pottery dishes. A big jar of fresh water stands in another corner. Clothing is folded over a bar set out from the wall. A doorway opens into a room where the corn is ground. Another opening in the center of the floor leads to a cool dark storage room below.

Everything has its place.

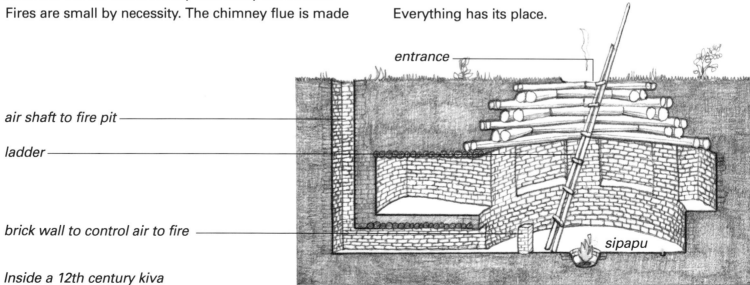

entrance

air shaft to fire pit

ladder

brick wall to control air to fire

sipapu

Kivas

Kivas were the ceremonial center of the community. All day long, men and boys came and went by ladder, gathering to weave, smoke, chat, practice complicated rituals and make ceremonial costumes. Although most kivas were restricted to male clan members, girls and women were allowed into some.

The Hopi of northeastern Arizona designed rectangular kivas. A third of the floor is raised as a stage. Women and visitors were sometimes allowed to sit there to watch ceremonies. The walls are plastered smooth and the room is heated by a woodstove.

A hole a few inches in diameter dug into the floor is the *sipapu*. It represents the opening in the earth through which the pueblo ancestors, guided by spirits, reached the surface. They believe this is how human beings came to inhabit the earth. Today, as in the past, kivas and the sipapu have a religious function as sacred as anything found in other religions.

Kivas can be identified by the long ladders extending out of their hatchways, high into the sky. This symbolizes the link of the present with the underworld.

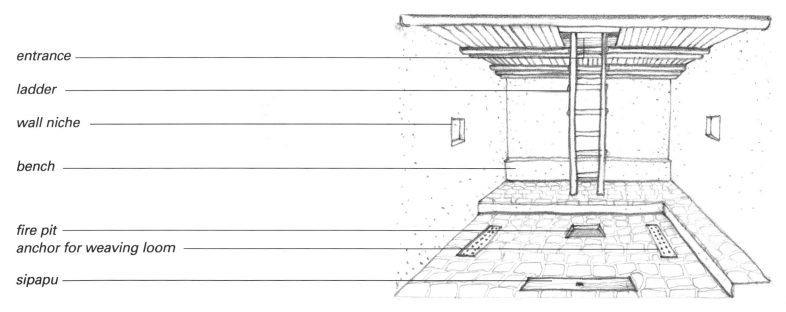

entrance

ladder

wall niche

bench

fire pit
anchor for weaving loom

sipapu

Many people have moved away from the old pueblos to live closer to work and schools. Those who continue to occupy the ancient sites now have electricity, glass in their windows and cars parked nearby. Over the centuries they have been affected by many influences: the Spanish, Roman Catholic missionaries, white Americans and other Native peoples. But the achievements of their ancestors remain an inspiration that encourages them to continue their sacred traditions.